# SPACE TORAH

## Astronaut Jeffrey Hoffman's
## Cosmic Mitzvah

by Rachelle Burk • illustrated by Craig Orback

INTERGALACTIC
Afikoman

SEATTLE

Jeff's head was often in the clouds. In Hebrew school, his teacher told stories about the Jewish people wandering in the desert, across oceans, to all corners of the world. But the stories Jeff told himself took him farther still—all the way to the stars.

On clear nights, Jeff loved looking through his family's telescope. The glowing moon and the shimmering stars made his heart race! He imagined rocketing through the galaxy like his favorite science fiction characters.

*Does life exist on other planets?* he wondered. *Will people ever really travel into outer space?*

Then, at age 16, Jeff watched in awe as Alan Shepard became the first American to journey into space. *That could be me one day,* he thought.

But in those days, only military pilots could become astronauts. Instead, Jeff became an astronomer, a scientist who studies the planets and stars.

Then, years later, he learned that NASA, the U.S. space agency, was seeking scientists like him to go into space. The dreams of his boyhood reawakened! Could this be his big chance? He went through months of interviews and tests.

When a big YES came from NASA in Houston, Jeff was over the moon with excitement. At last, he would travel among the stars!

In 1985 Jeff blasted into orbit for the first time. As the shuttle *Discovery* zoomed to outer space, he gazed out the window at the glowing Earth.

The splendor of blue oceans, green mountains, white polar ice, and dazzling lightning storms left him breathless.

During a quiet moment, Jeff unfolded a handwritten prayer. He silently read the words that expressed his thanks to God, and his hope for a safe mission.

"Praised art thou, who stretches forth the heaven and lays the foundation of the Earth . . ."

All went well until one of the satellites they deployed failed to start. This was not part of the plan! Yet, Jeff was prepared. His heart pounded as he suited up and exited the shuttle. Such exhilaration, to float weightless between the Earth and the stars!

He felt peaceful and free in the silence,
but also alone. Was God here with him?

On each of his next four missions, Jeff honored
his Jewish heritage by carrying symbols of his faith:

his Bar Mitzvah
prayer book,

a mezuzah that he attached
to the wall of his bunk,

and even a dreidel, which he
spun—suspended in midair—
to celebrate Hanukkah.

With each orbit around the Earth, Jeff felt more connected to the universe.

He talked about his heavenly adventures with his rabbi, who was also his friend. As the rabbi listened, he imagined that Jeff's view from space might be how God saw the world. This gave him an idea.

"God sent the Torah—the most sacred Jewish object—from heaven. Why not bring the Torah back 'home' for a visit?" the rabbi suggested.

*The Torah in space?* Jeff loved the idea of a Sabbath celebration among the stars. But this was impossible. Astronauts could only bring personal items that would fit in a kit the size of a lunchbox. A Torah scroll is as big as a suitcase! It would be far too large to take on the space shuttle.

That's when the rabbi launched a mission of his own: to find a miniature Torah for Jeff. He finally located three small, handwritten scrolls. Which one should make the celestial journey?

Jeff envisioned children eager to read from a little Torah that had orbited the planet.

So the rabbi asked young Hebrew school students to help with the selection.

They chose the scroll with the easiest Hebrew handwriting to read.

Jeff's congregation raised enough money to purchase the tiny Torah, and soon it was on its way to Houston.

On February 22, 1996, the shuttle *Columbia* rocketed into space.

Halfway through the mission, while most of the crew members slept, Jeff watched the sun rise over his planet.

It was Shabbat evening back home in Texas,

and Shabbat morning in Jerusalem.

Floating in zero gravity, Jeff unrolled his chosen portion of the Torah. The section felt just right for this historic mitzvah—the first Torah reading beyond the boundaries of Earth. Orbiting Earth at 17,400 miles per hour, Jeff began to read from the Book of Genesis—the story of Creation.

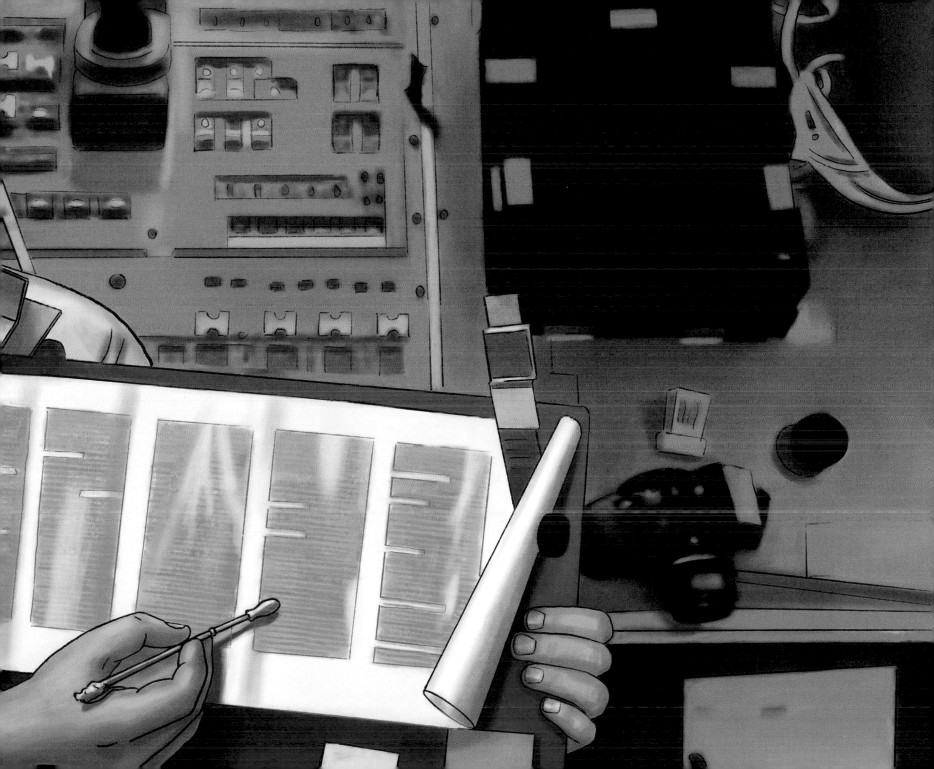

God created the heavens and the Earth.

A generation of children have read and learned from the Space Torah in the years since Jeff performed his cosmic mitzvah.

Taking the Torah into orbit only deepened his love of space. He still marvels at the wonders of the universe.

"Wherever Jews have wandered, they have carried the Torah with them," he says.

Jeff just happens to have wandered farther than most.

# AFTERWORD by Jeff Hoffman

I have brought many objects into space and given them to friends and family as "space souvenirs"—banners from my high school and university, a flag from my son's Boy Scout troop, gold and silver medallions with our flight logos, and so on. People like the idea of having something that has been in space, and one of the mezuzahs I took into space now graces the doorpost of the Jerusalem Science Museum.

I look at the Space Torah differently from other objects I have taken with me into space. A Torah is a sacred object, and you cannot make it more sacred or more holy by bringing it into space. For me, bringing a Torah into space and performing a ritual by reading the initial בְּרֵאשִׁית (Beresheet) portion brought the holiness of the Torah into space. It made space more special.

For me, space travel represents the future, and taking a Torah into space was an affirmation that our Jewish tradition, which goes back to antiquity, will continue into the future. Passing the tradition from one generation to another is the Jewish concept of **L'dor V'dor**. I am happy that this book makes the story of the Space Torah accessible to many other young children who do not have physical access to the Space Torah.

The tradition continues . . . *L'DOR V'DOR.*

# AUTHOR'S NOTE by Rachelle Burk

**Dr. Jeffrey Alan Hoffman** flew on five NASA space missions between 1985 and 1996. He logged more than 1,200 hours and 21.5 million miles over 50 days in orbit. He was the third Jewish astronaut in space, after Russian cosmonaut Boris Volynov (1969) and American Judith Resnik (1984). Jeff was the first to bring Jewish artifacts on space missions.

Jeff faced a number of problems when planning his cosmic mitzvah. First, how would he determine the start of the Sabbath, since the sun rises and sets every 90 minutes in space? He decided to begin the Torah reading when it would be the start of the Sabbath in Houston (Friday at sundown) and Sabbath day in Jerusalem (Saturday morning).

Second, Jeff initially planned to read the traditional weekly Torah portion. However, it would be impossible to know with certainty which portion to prepare since launch dates are often delayed. He decided that, since this would be the first Torah reading in space, he should start at the beginning. Genesis—the Story of Creation—seemed a perfect choice.

Finally, how would he secure the Torah in order to read it in the zero-gravity conditions of space? His solution was to separate his chosen pages from the Torah before it went into orbit. Jeff carefully cut the threads to remove the pages, which he then rolled into a specially designed silver tube. He stored the rest of the scroll (without its handles) in another part of the shuttle for safety. When he began the Torah reading, Jeff clipped the section to a board to keep it from floating away. Once the shuttle returned to Earth, a scribe sewed the sheets back into the Torah during a special ceremony.

Jeff asked fellow astronaut Claude Nicollier to videotape his Torah reading. He intended it as a private mitzvah that he would share with his family and synagogue upon his return. Twenty years later, Rachel Raz, a Boston educator and entrepreneur, heard Jeff speak about the event. She wanted to share it with the world. In 2020, Raz and Verissima Productions released an independent short film titled *Space Torah* (www.SpaceTorahProject.com).

The Space Torah still resides with Jeff's former congregation near the NASA Johnson Space Center in Houston, Texas. Little silver space shuttles adorn the scroll handles. Adults who otherwise are not strong enough to hold a full-size Torah can participate in prayer rituals by carrying the seven-by-four-inch miniature Torah. Most joyfully, a multitude of children continue to celebrate their Bar/Bat Mitzvahs by reading from the historic celestial scroll. To Jeff, and to his Houston congregation, the Space Torah symbolizes a connection with the past and a vision toward the future.

# GLOSSARY OF JEWISH WORDS

**Bar Mitzvah:** A Jewish coming-of-age ritual for boys. Bat Mitzvah is the equivalent for girls.

**Dreidel:** A small four-sided spinning top used in a children's game, traditionally played during the Jewish festival of Hanukkah.

**Genesis:** The first book of the Hebrew Bible, which tells the story of the world's creation.

**Hanukkah:** The Jewish Festival of Lights. The holiday lasts for eight nights and usually occurs in December. It celebrates a military victory of the Jews over foreign rulers.

**L'dor V'dor:** Hebrew for "from generation to generation," which is understood as the concept of passing Jewish values, rituals, traditions, and history to the next generation.

**Mezuzah:** A scroll containing prayers from the Hebrew Bible that is held in a decorative case. It is traditionally attached to the doorpost to identify a Jewish home.

**Mitzvah:** A good deed or religious duty.

**Scribe:** In Judaism, a person who handwrites the Torah in Hebrew and sews the pages together.

**Shabbat:** The Jewish Sabbath; the day of the week for rest and worship, beginning at sundown Friday and ending at sundown Saturday.

**Torah:** The sacred scroll that contains all the recorded Jewish laws; the first five books of the Hebrew Bible.

# GLOSSARY OF SCIENCE WORDS

**NASA:** National Aeronautics and Space Administration, the organization in charge of U.S. science and technology related to airplanes or space.

**Space shuttle:** A rocket-launched spacecraft used to make repeated journeys between the Earth and Earth's orbit.

**Zero gravity:** A condition of weightlessness, as of a body in orbit, when the effect of gravity is absent.

# ABOUT THE AUTHOR

**Rachelle Burk** writes fiction and nonfiction for children ages 3–12.

Among her other Jewish-themed picture books are *She's a Mensch! Jewish Women Who Rocked the World*, *A Mitzvah for George Washington*, *Matzah Ball Chase*, and *The Best Four Questions* (a 2019 PJ Library selection). She has also published many secular titles, and has written for magazines such as *Highlights* and *Scholastic SuperScience*.

A retired social worker, Rachelle is also a children's entertainer, performing as Tickles the Clown and Mother Goof Storyteller. She loves to share her love of reading and writing by visiting elementary schools around the country. You can find out more about her books and school visits at RachelleBurk.com.

# ABOUT THE ARTIST

**Craig Orback** is the illustrator of over 20 published books for children, including *Starring Steven Spielberg: The Making of a Young Filmmaker*, *Born to Draw Comics: The Story of Charles Schulz and the Creation of Peanuts,* and the Charlotte Award and Keystone to Reading Book Award winning title *The Can Man*. Craig loves to share his books with students during school and library visits. He lives near Seattle, WA, where you can find him adventuring with his son in the beautiful Pacific Northwest. He invites you to visit him online at www.craigorback.com.

# ACKNOWLEDGMENTS

With boundless admiration and galactic thanks to **Dr. Jeffrey Alan Hoffman**, for being so down to earth while indulging my infinite questions during phone calls and emails. You are a star!

My enormous gratitude to **Rabbi Shaul Osadchey**, for your answers and insights, and especially for the guided tour of Or Ami during my visit to Houston to see the Space Torah.

*Toda raba* to **Rachel Raz** for your kindness, help, and Zoom screenings of the inspiring film *Space Torah*. And, of course, for the personal introductions that launched the writing of this book.

*Going into space did not make the Torah more special,
the Torah made space more special.*

~Dr. Jeffrey Hoffman

*For Fred: I love you to the stars and back.*

~Rachelle Burk

*For my son Lewis. I love you to outer space and back!*

~Craig Orback

Text Copyright 2024 Rachelle Burk
Illustrations Copyright 2024 Intergalactic Afikoman
Designed by Elynn Cohen

Intergalactic Afikoman
1037 NE 65th Street #164
Seattle, Washington 98115

Publisher's Cataloging-in-Publication

Burk, Rachelle, author. | Orback, Craig, illustrator.

Space Torah : astronaut Jeffrey Hoffman's cosmic mitzvah / by Rachelle Burk ; illustrated by Craig Orback.

First edition. | Seattle : Intergalactic Afikoman, [2024] | Interest age level: 004-008. | Summary: As an astronaut, he journeyed far beyond them. On his final mission, Jeff brought a miniature Torah into orbit for an out-of-this-world Shabbat celebration!—Publisher.

ISBN: 978-1-951365-19-6

LCSH: Hoffman, Jeffrey A.—Juvenile literature. | Astronauts—United States—Biography—Juvenile literature. | Bible. Pentateuch—Juvenile literature. | Sabbath—Juvenile literature. | Space flight—Juvenile literature. | CYAC: Hoffman, Jeffrey A. | Astronauts—United States—Biography. | Bible. Pentateuch. | Sabbath. | Space flight. | LCGFT: Biographies. | BISAC: JUVENILE NONFICTION / Biography & Autobiography / Science & Technology. | JUVENILE NONFICTION / Religion / Judaism.

LCC: TL789.85.H64 B87 2024 | DDC: 629.450092--dc23

Library of Congress Control Number: 2023945728

Printed in the USA
First Edition

10   9   8   7   6   5   4   3   2   1